ELIZABETH II
PRINCESS, QUEEN, ICON

ELIZABETH II
PRINCESS, QUEEN, ICON

INTRODUCTION BY ALEXANDRA SHULMAN

NATIONAL PORTRAIT GALLERY, LONDON

CONTENTS

ELIZABETH II
PRINCESS, QUEEN, ICON

Alexandra Shulman

Alexandra Shulman is a British journalist and former Editor-in-Chief of British Vogue. She is the author of *Clothes... and Other Things That Matter* (2020) and *Inside Vogue: My Diary Of Vogue's 100th Year* (2016), and was a Trustee of the National Portrait Gallery from 1999 to 2007.

It is a curious fact that in today's image-conscious world, where every one of us is able to produce pictures of ourselves adjusted to our idealised requirements, the person who has been the subject of the most images of all is a 95-year-old woman who has probably never fiddled around with an Instagram filter or Photoshop.

HM Queen Elizabeth II, born in 1926, has lived through the greatest changes in the creation of images of any monarch in the history of the world. Aside from the traditional painted portraits and drawings that were for centuries the method of royalty publicly positioning themselves, she has also had photography, television, social media, the 24-hour news cycle and the visual scrutiny of a massively enlarged world communication network with which to contend. And much of this is not in her control. Since she was born, there has been scarcely any element of her life that has not been recorded by somebody else, from the postcard of her as a sweet baby girl in an adorable bonnet (fig. 1) to the immensely tragic pictures beamed around the world of her seated alone, due to pandemic restrictions, in St George's Chapel, Windsor Castle, at the funeral of Prince Philip, her husband of seventy-three years.

The majority of pictures in this collection show us the Queen in a formally documented manner and, because they are deliberately arranged and sanctioned, they provide a fascinating insight into how she – or in the very early images, her parents – wished her to be seen. Even the more spontaneous early photographs, such as the 1936 Studio Lisa shot that shows us how early on in her life the Queen's passion for corgis began, would have been subject to a rigorous editing process (fig. 2).

All these representations of the Queen can tell us so much of the time in which they were created and what the monarchy wanted us to feel about them. It has often been said that part of the key to the Queen's success in her role throughout her long reign is that she has so clearly made public service and an overriding sense of duty the mainstay. But, when you look at so many of the pictures here, you see how they are about something else too. Something more emotional. They are attempts at connecting us to this family, which needs to be both relatable and yet something quite other.

The task of being at once symbolic and human is not simple, and this is true now more than ever when we crave, and perhaps expect, a sense of intimacy. So much contemporary documentation of famous people is intended to look as if it were the 'real' person, even if in reality the image is as much a construct as a Cecil Beaton portrait. Our expectations of what we are allowed to see has changed. No longer is the distant monarch entirely satisfactory, nor can she be just like us. Images of the Queen, in a way that is not so distant from fashion photographs, need to be aspirational. She has to appear just the right, attainable side of perfect. But, unlike a fashion photograph, we need to believe and trust in her.

What is striking about the thousands of images of the Queen over her ninety-five years of life is how consistent they are. The ingredients of what and who we have come to recognise as the Queen were established even by the time she was 10 years old, when Princess Elizabeth became unexpectedly heir presumptive to the throne. In the earliest Marcus Adams 1929 portrait (see p. 23), she already wears the pearl necklace that has forever been her trademark jewellery. The pearls may have graduated from the little seed pearls of childhood to fabulous double and triple strands, but they are always with her. Her hair has never changed from the wavy chin-length

[FIG. 2]
'PRINCESS ELIZABETH WITH HER CORGI DOOKIE'
THE GARDEN OF 145 PICCADILLY, LONDON
STUDIO LISA (LISA SHERIDAN), JULY 1936

Modern gelatin silver print, 132 x 96mm
NPG x199577

cut, swept back from her brow to show her clear and steady gaze. Similarly, when you consider how much our own clothes change with the decades, hers have remained strikingly similar and yet, despite that, never contemporary nor old fashioned.

Well into her fifties, she favoured a silhouette inspired by the post-war New Look of Christian Dior – a fitted bodice, narrow waist and wide skirt. Like many, she retained a fondness for the fashions of the period when she was a young woman. Even her off-duty clothes follow suit; she often wears a waist-length twinset, a tailored tweed jacket, and an A-line skirt or a kilt, as in David Montgomery's image of her in the countryside trailed by her faithful prop, her corgis (fig. 3). The Queen may not always be hugely interested in fashion, but she has always cared about her clothes, in recent years taking pleasure in matching her patterned dresses to the bright fabric of her coats, and always accessorising every outfit with the astounding collections of diamond

[FIG. 3]
'QUEEN ELIZABETH WITH CORGIS (COUNTRY)'
BALMORAL CASTLE, ABERDEENSHIRE
DAVID MONTGOMERY, 1967

Digital chromogenic print, 355 x 455mm
NPG x201263

brooches she owns. And such a signature style has
served her well, helping her live up to expectations. As
a monarch, her clothes have always had to conform to
regal demands – to allow her to be seen from a distance,
to be functional and not to disappoint. People want to
see the Queen and they want her to look as they expect.
Distinctive and utterly familiar.

So many of the memorable portraits of the Queen
portray her in ceremonial costume, a million miles
away from her personal style and yet at the same
time so much a part of how we imagine her: the
coronation robe with its ermine-edged velvet mantle
and embroidered emblems of the United Kingdom
and Commonwealth; the heavy dark skirt she wore
to ride side-saddle for many years at the Trooping of
the Colour; the blue garter sash of so many formal
portraits; the cloaks of the stern Annigoni painting
(fig. 4) and the Cecil Beaton and Annie Leibovitz
photographs; and, of course, the incredible bejeweled
crowns. At such moments, she is draped in what
Valerie Cummings describes as 'Ruritanian glamour'
in her excellent book, *Royal Dress*. She is symbolic, out
of this world, a distanced figure clad in the panoply
of royalty. In more recent years, we have seen the
Queen presented in this manner far less often, but,
even in a more everyday mode, she loses none of her
majesty. She remains one of the contemporary world's
true icons, so many ideas and ideals projected onto
her being, and being there. What has changed is the
varying culture of the times.

As Princess Elizabeth reached adulthood, the
country was at war and it could be said that in some
ways the royal family had a 'good' war. Still recovering
from the epic shock of the abdication of Edward VIII,
the Second World War gave George VI and his family

[FIG. 4]
QUEEN ELIZABETH II
PIETRO ANNIGONI, 1969

Tempera grassa on paper on panel,
1981 x 1778mm
NPG 4706

an opportunity to establish themselves in the minds of the public. They were reassuring figures during this time of crisis and needed to be seen, which they were mainly through the many photographs they released in those years. We have Princesses Elizabeth and Margaret in 1940 in front of their broadcasting microphones (fig. 5), dressed identically in neat wool jackets and unthreateningly normal striped jerseys, Elizabeth with the script in her hand. She was launching a voice to go alongside the pictures.

In the year of Elizabeth's seventeenth birthday, Dorothy Wilding photographed her in a knitted jumper, the uniform of a Sea Ranger which she had registered for pre-service (fig. 6). A year earlier, she had become Colonel of the Grenadier Guards, commemorated by a Beaton portrait wearing their insignia (see p. 33). And there is a War Office photograph of 1945 where, dressed in boiler suit and

tie, she posed against the kind of military vehicle she was learning to service as part of the messaging that, like the rest of the country, she was engaged in the war effort (see pp. 34–5).

It shows a dramatic change from the carefree girl of childhood in the photographs of Studio Lisa, who we never really see again. For, by the time the war is over, she almost immediately becomes a wife, a mother and then the Queen. In 1945, Cecil Beaton, so often employed as court photographer, wrote in his diaries, 'Princess Elizabeth's easy charm, like her mother's, does not carry across in her photographs and each time one sees her one is delighted to find how much more serene, magnetic and at the same time meltingly sympathetic she is than one had imagined.' What a trial it must be to have had to spend countless hours of your life posing for portraits, to know that your every glance on walkabouts and in audiences will be analysed and captured. No wonder she sometimes appears lacking in 'easy charm'. Nonetheless, she has more than lived up to the challenge and on occasion, as in the Jane Bown and David Bailey portraits of later years (see pp. 124–5 and p. 135), has allowed the dry sense of humour she is known for to seep through.

My personal favourite in this collection is a lightweight image compared to the many here of such great moment. The photograph was taken on the Royal Yacht *Britannia* in 1971 by Patrick Lichfield, a distant cousin and family friend of the Queen (fig. 7). It is a snapshot at a candlelit dinner where the Queen is flanked by two handsome men in summer shirts. She is so clearly having a delightful time, wearing a sleeveless evening dress, a dab of coral lipstick and, although on a boat, an enormous, beautiful diamond necklace. She is in her mid-forties and would have

[FIG. 6]
QUEEN ELIZABETH II
DOROTHY WILDING, 1943

Half-plate film negative
NPG x34338

[FIG. 7]
QUEEN ELIZABETH II
HER MAJESTY'S YACHT _BRITANNIA_
PATRICK LICHFIELD, 1971

Cibachrome print, 207 x 296mm
NPG x29567

been monarch for eighteen years. That evening she would have had no idea that fifty-one years later she would still be on the throne and the most popular member of her family. Nor could she have imagined the many scandals, vicissitudes and dramas that were yet to come, let alone the way the whole world would change dramatically in its attitudes to history and legacy, and indeed royalty. No, she knows none of that, and it is enchanting just to see a moment where she looks so at peace with it all.

PRINCESS

Princess Elizabeth of York was born on 21 April 1926 in London, England. As a young royal, countless images were made of her throughout her childhood as she grew up alongside her sister Margaret (see p. 24) and took part in early royal duties (see p. 27). When her father George VI became king in 1936 after the abdication of her uncle Edward VIII, Elizabeth became heir to the throne. Portraits from this period show the princess taking on new royal duties while starting her own family, marrying Prince Philip in 1947 (see p. 41) and becoming a mother to the couple's first child Prince Charles in 1948.

[2]
'THE DUKE AND DUCHESS OF YORK
PHOTOGRAPHED WITH THE INFANT PRINCESS
ON THE DAY OF THE CHRISTENING'
PUBLISHED BY RAPHAEL TUCK & SONS,
29 MAY 1926

Postcard print, 139 x 89mm
NPG x193257

Marcus Adams took the first official photographs of the future Queen Mother and Queen Elizabeth II in 1926 and continued photographing the royal family up until 1956, recording the Queen's life from her infancy to her becoming a monarch and mother herself. Widely acclaimed for his photographic portraits of children, Adams' studio at 43 Dover Street in Mayfair was filled with toys and featured a camera disguised as a toy cabinet to make his young subjects feel at ease. Adams' photographs of the princess document numerous early official portraits of the young royal and are key early examples of how her image developed as her royal roles changed.

[3]
PRINCESS ELIZABETH
MARCUS ADAMS, 30 JULY 1929

Gelatin silver print, 368 x 292mm
NPG P140(19)

[4]
**PRINCESS ELIZABETH AND
PRINCESS MARGARET**
ST PAUL'S WALDEN BURY, HERTFORDSHIRE
FREDERICK THURSTON, AUGUST 1932

Gelatin silver print, 159 x 208mm
NPG x87179

[5]
**'H.R.H. THE PRINCESS ELIZABETH:
HER ROYAL HIGHNESS'S MERRY SMILE'**
PUBLISHED J. BEAGLES & CO, c.1933

Postcard print, 139 x 89mm
NPG x193144

[6]
***MARION CRAWFORD, PRINCESS ELIZABETH
AND PRINCESS MARGARET***
QUEEN ELIZABETH, 1930s

Gelatin silver print, 206 x 254mm
NPG x194475

[7]
***KING GEORGE VI, PRINCESS MARGARET,
PRINCESS ELIZABETH AND QUEEN ELIZABETH***
THRONE ROOM, BUCKINGHAM PALACE,
LONDON
DOROTHY WILDING, 1937

Cream-toned gelatin silver print, 293 x 229mm
NPG x25287

This royal group portrait was taken at Buckingham Palace shortly before the outbreak of war and soon after the coronation of George VI. During the war years, the king and his family were a powerful symbol of national unity and stability. George VI brought to the monarchy at a crucial time an innate good sense, great courage and an unswerving sense of duty while the Second World War and its after-effects overshadowed his whole reign. This portrait of the royal family includes their pet corgi Dookie, who was lured into the composition with a biscuit placed on the king's shoe. Photographer Marcus Adams encountered considerable technical problems when creating this image. It had to be photographed with a very wide aperture, which put the background out of focus. Adams therefore took a second photograph of the background alone, bleached out the background in the first negative, bound the two negatives together and printed from his double negative.

[8]
PRINCESS ELIZABETH, KING GEORGE VI,
QUEEN ELIZABETH AND PRINCESS MARGARET
BUCKINGHAM PALACE, LONDON
MARCUS ADAMS, 1938

Gelatin silver print, 357 x 260mm
NPG P140(13)

In contrast to official portraits, Studio Lisa's more relaxed and informal images capture the royals in their residences at Windsor, 145 Piccadilly, and Balmoral Castle, away from the trappings of ceremonial life. The princesses are photographed pursuing their favourite pastimes – sketching, painting, performing pantomimes and playing games in the garden. The family's pet corgis enjoyed an important role in the children's lives, and find their way into these photographs too (see p. 8). Sheridan witnessed an 'affectionate, united family' and recalled being 'impressed by the informality of their home lives and by their unaffected charm'. Her images depict a childhood not so far removed from children of a similar age throughout the country. Over thirty years, husband-and-wife team Lisa and Jimmy Sheridan recorded thirteen photographic sessions with three generations of the royal family, including photographing the Queen with her own children at Windsor Castle.

[9]
PRINCESS ELIZABETH
STUDIO LISA (LISA SHERIDAN), 1941

Cibachrome print, 267 x 331mm
NPG x35388

[10]
'PRINCESS ELIZABETH AS COLONEL-IN-CHIEF OF THE GRENADIER GUARDS'
CECIL BEATON, 1942

Gelatin silver print, 348 x 297mm
NPG x20203

[11]

PRINCESS ELIZABETH
AUXILIARY TERRITORIAL SERVICE
TRAINING CENTRE, CAMBERLEY, SURREY
WILLIAM HORTON, 1945

Cibachrome print, 246 x 332mm
NPG x35391

[12]
PRINCESS ELIZABETH
CECIL BEATON, 15 NOVEMBER 1945

Gelatin silver contact print, 251 x 200mm
NPG x26023

QUEEN ELIZABETH, PRINCESS MARGARET,
PRINCESS ELIZABETH AND KING GEORGE VI
BOW ROOM, BUCKINGHAM PALACE, LONDON
DOROTHY WILDING, 27 MAY 1946

Gelatin silver print, 324 x 414mm
NPG x25238

**PRINCESS ELIZABETH; JAN CHRISTIAN SMUTS,
PRIME MINISTER OF SOUTH AFRICA;
KING GEORGE VI; QUEEN ELIZABETH; AND
PRINCESS MARGARET**
SOUTH AFRICA DURING A ROYAL TOUR
NATAL MERCURY, 1947

Gelatin silver print, 104 x 165mm
NPG x20699

[15]
PRINCE PHILIP AND
PRINCESS ELIZABETH
DOROTHY WILDING, JULY 1947

Half-plate film negative
NPG x37999

Sir James Gunn's post-war portrait shows King George VI, Queen Elizabeth, Princess Elizabeth and Princess Margaret at tea. Throughout the Second World War, the royal family remained in London, and their determination to share in the fate of the nation increased the monarchy's popularity. This portrait was an official commission for the National Portrait Gallery, and, in representing the very British ritual of afternoon tea, it manages to be both patriotic and informal, and is reflective of changing perceptions of the monarchy. Gunn had been chosen by the king and queen for the commission, and recalled the difficulty of placing the corgi, moving it about on the canvas in a paper cut-out.

[20]
'CONVERSATION PIECE AT THE ROYAL LODGE, WINDSOR'
SIR JAMES GUNN, 1950

Oil on canvas, 1511 x 1003mm
NPG 3778

[21]
PRINCESS MARGARET, PRINCESS ANNE AND
PRINCESS ELIZABETH, DUCHESS OF EDINBURGH
BALMORAL CASTLE, ABERDEENSHIRE
UNKNOWN PHOTOGRAPHER, 1951

Gelatin silver print, 83 x 56mm
NPG x35704

[22]
'THE ROYAL FAMILY'
YOUSUF KARSH, 1951

Gelatin silver print, 273 x 352mm
NPG P347

QUEEN

Following the death of George VI on 6 February 1952, Elizabeth ascended the throne. Her coronation took place just over a year later on 2 June 1953 at Westminster Abbey, London. From the beginning of her reign, portraits of Elizabeth took on the new purpose of representing the ruling monarch. Images including Beaton's coronation portrait (p. 65) document important events in royal history, while candid photographs such as those by Studio Lisa (p. 74) capture day-to-day moments outside of official duties. The portraits in this section work together to present a multifaceted picture of the new Queen in the early years of her reign.

[23]
QUEEN ELIZABETH II
DOROTHY WILDING, 26 FEBRUARY 1952

Gelatin silver print, 445 x 343mm
NPG x34844

Dorothy Wilding first photographed Elizabeth
in 1937 at the coronation of her father, King
George VI (see p. 27), and subsequently made
portraits of her on significant occasions. Wilding
was the first woman photographer to be granted
'by appointment' status to the royal family.
This portrait was one of a series made to mark
the Queen's accession in 1952 and coronation
in 1953. Elizabeth posed for the photographer
fifty-nine times wearing gowns by Norman
Hartnell. Copies of the best images were sent to
every embassy in the world and were the most
memorable images of the Queen at least until
her Silver Jubilee. Studies from this sitting also
formed the basis for the new currency, appearing
on banknotes and millions of stamps. Other
portraits from this sitting (see pp. 60–1) feature
colour applied by hand to Wilding's photograph.
The hand-coloured images are at once more
naturalistic than the monochrome original
and also more artificial. Naturalism and artifice
are themes that run through the subsequent
iconography of the Queen.

[24]
QUEEN ELIZABETH II
PHOTOGRAPHER'S STUDIO, LONDON
DOROTHY WILDING, 26 FEBRUARY 1952

Chlorobromide print on tissue and card mount,
290 x 215mm
NPG P870(5)

[25]
QUEEN ELIZABETH II
DOROTHY WILDING, HAND-COLOURED
BY HER ASSISTANT BEATRICE JOHNSON,
15 APRIL 1952

Hand-coloured gelatin silver print, 316 x 248mm
NPG x125105

[26]
QUEEN ELIZABETH II
PHOTOGRAPHER'S STUDIO, LONDON
DOROTHY WILDING, HAND-COLOURED
BY HER ASSISTANT BEATRICE JOHNSON, 26
FEBRUARY 1952

Hand-coloured gelatin silver print, 306 x 252mm
NPG x34846

Cecil Beaton's photographs of the royal family were central to shaping the monarchy's public image for over three decades. His early portraits made use of painted backdrops, sumptuous gowns and fresh flowers picked from his garden to picture the young princess (see p. 37). Only eight years later, at the age of 27, Elizabeth was transformed into a powerful monarch, with an estimated audience of twenty-seven million people watching her coronation on television in 1953. Beaton received the 'coveted invitation' to take the Queen's official coronation portrait. Photographed in full regalia in the Green Drawing Room at Buckingham Palace after the ceremony, she was posed against a backdrop of Henry VII's chapel in Westminster Abbey, wearing the Imperial State Crown, in which the Black Prince's Ruby and Elizabeth I's pearl earrings are set. Beaton's impression of the new Queen was of an individual 'cool, smiling, sovereign of the situation'. After wearing the crown for three hours, she was asked a question by Beaton and is said to have responded, 'Yes, the Crown does get rather heavy.'

[28]
QUEEN ELIZABETH II
GREEN DRAWING ROOM, BUCKINGHAM PALACE, LONDON
CECIL BEATON, 2 JUNE 1953

Semi-matte cibachrome print, 331 x 249mm
NPG x35390

[29]
QUEEN ELIZABETH II
LONDON, UNITED KINGDOM
PUBLISHED BY RAPHAEL TUCK & SONS, c.1951

Postcard print, 139 x 90mm
NPG x193039

The Queen is shown speaking to Marilyn Monroe, who attended the Royal Command Performance of Powell and Pressburger's war film *The Battle of the River Plate* at the Empire Cinema in Leicester Square. The Queen and Monroe briefly discussed being temporary neighbours. In this photograph, Monroe is wearing a gold lamé gown and is standing between Victor Mature and Anthony Quayle, who starred in the film.

[30]
QUEEN ELIZABETH II, VICTOR MATURE,
MARILYN MONROE AND ANTHONY QUAYLE
EMPIRE CINEMA, LEICESTER SQUARE, LONDON
UNKNOWN PHOTOGRAPHER FOR *DAILY MIRROR*,
29 OCTOBER 1956

Modern gelatin silver print, 188 x 242mm
NPG x136606

Antony Armstrong-Jones, later Lord Snowdon, began his professional career in 1951 as assistant to the society photographer Baron, and opened his own studio on Pimlico Road, London, in 1953. He photographed the Queen, Prince Philip and their two eldest children in the gardens of Buckingham Palace in 1957. Only twenty minutes were available for the sitting, so he planned it carefully in advance, submitting sketches of compositions for approval. Here, Princess Anne is shown reading a book with her mother, to emphasise the monarch's family values. The following year he met the Queen's sister, Princess Margaret, and the two were married in 1960, after which he was granted the title 'First Earl of Snowdon'.

[31]
QUEEN ELIZABETH II AND PRINCESS ANNE
BUCKINGHAM PALACE, LONDON
LORD SNOWDON, 10 OCTOBER 1957

Gelatin silver print, 508 x 404mm
NPG P1639

[32]
QUEEN ELIZABETH II
DONALD MCKAGUE, DECEMBER 1958

Chromogenic print, 425 x 335mm
NPG P1583

The American photojournalist Eve Arnold's
startlingly spontaneous photograph
emphasises the Queen's sense of fun
and, in contrast to conventional portraits,
approachability. Arnold joined Magnum
Photos in 1951, and, after moving to Britain
in the early 1960s, she worked for the
Sunday Times and began to use colour
as part of her practice.

[39]
QUEEN ELIZABETH II
EVE ARNOLD, 1968

Cibachrome print, 432 x 295mm
NPG P520

[4 0]

'CHRISTMAS AT WINDSOR CASTLE, DECORATING THE TREE'
STATE APARTMENTS AT WINDSOR CASTLE,
BERKSHIRE, DURING THE FILMING OF
THE DOCUMENTARY *ROYAL FAMILY*
JOAN WILLIAMS, 1969

Chromogenic print, 195 x 245mm
NPG x199582

[41]
QUEEN ELIZABETH II
PIETRO ANNIGONI, 1969

Tempera grassa on paper on panel,
1981 x 1778mm
NPG 4706

QUEEN ELIZABETH II
BALMORAL CASTLE, ABERDEENSHIRE
PATRICK LICHFIELD, 1971

Cibachrome print, 386 x 258mm
NPG x29571

A cousin of the Queen, Patrick Lichfield was an established society and fashion photographer when he was invited to photograph the Queen's tour of the Far East in 1971 on board Her Majesty's Yacht *Britannia*. Lichfield's informal photographs offer glimpses into the daily life of the royal family on the yacht. He presents a relaxed monarch at dinner (see p. 13), or working intently with her Private Secretary to review and sign documents well after midnight. This image shows Elizabeth II on board *Britannia* after it had crossed the equator. Lichfield, having been ducked by the crew to mark this passage, used a waterproof camera to capture her amused reaction. Among informal images of the Queen, it is one of the more spontaneous.

[43]
QUEEN ELIZABETH II
HER MAJESTY'S YACHT *BRITANNIA*
PATRICK LICHFIELD, 1971

Cibachrome print, 386 x 258mm
NPG x29562

[44]
'QUEEN ELIZABETH II AND HER FAMILY'
PATRICK LICHFIELD, SUMMER 1971

Chromogenic print, 387 x 490mm
NPG P1578

**'QUEEN ELIZABETH II VISITS THE SILVERWOOD
COLLIERY IN YORKSHIRE'**
ANDREW DAVIDSON FOR CAMERA PRESS, 1975

Gelatin silver print, 253 x 176mm
NPG x134734

[47]
QUEEN ELIZABETH II
DENNIS CONSTANTINE, 12 JULY 1978

Chromogenic print, 498 x 396mm
NPG P1521

The *Royal Family* documentary was first
aired on BBC One and ITV in 1969, and
presented insight into a year in the lives
of the Queen and her family, attracting an
audience of over thirty million viewers.
Joan Williams, a photographer for the BBC,
captured behind-the-scenes images during
the making of the documentary for use in
the press. Over twenty-three years, Williams
continued to document many royal events
for the BBC, including state visits and the
Queen's Christmas broadcasts. Here, Sir
David Attenborough, formerly BBC Two
Controller and Director of BBC Programmes,
is photographed by Williams filming the
Christmas Message with the Queen in the
Royal Mews at Buckingham Palace.

[48]
**SIR DAVID ATTENBOROUGH AND
QUEEN ELIZABETH II**
BUCKINGHAM PALACE, LONDON
JOAN WILLIAMS, 1986

Chromogenic print, 191 x 241mm
NPG x200326

ICON

The public image of Elizabeth II continued to develop as her reign progressed. New portraits emerged that encompassed the historical and cultural shifts taking place in the later part of the twentieth century and at the start of the twenty-first century. Artists such as Andy Warhol (pp. 107–9) and Hiroshi Sugimoto (p. 115) used new techniques to incorporate her representation in their works that result in a sense of timelessness. As the Queen's rule became record-breaking, these new portraits spoke to the longevity of her reign and contributed to the cultivation of her iconic status in modern culture and history globally.

This set of four iconic portraits of the Queen held in the Gallery Collections (opposite and pp. 108–9) are by American artist and film-maker Andy Warhol, who once said 'I want to be as famous as the Queen of England'. The set is part of a series entitled *Reigning Queens*, which included portraits of Queen Margarethe of Denmark, Queen Beatrix of the Netherlands and Queen Ntombi of Swaziland, and alludes to some of Warhol's favourite themes including celebrity, class and consumerism. The portrait of Queen Elizabeth II is derived from an official 1977 Jubilee photograph by Peter Grugeon, but the screen-printed images transformed the Queen's features through the introduction of graphic shapes and exaggerated, unexpected colour. In the resulting images, she is at once instantly recognisable but utterly unknowable.

[49]
QUEEN ELIZABETH II
ANDY WARHOL, 1985

Silkscreen print, 1000 x 800mm
NPG 5882(3)

[50]
QUEEN ELIZABETH II
ANDY WARHOL, 1985

Silkscreen print, 1000 x 800mm
NPG 5882(2)

[51]
QUEEN ELIZABETH II
ANDY WARHOL, 1985

Silkscreen print, 1000 x 800mm
NPG 5882(1)

[52]
QUEEN ELIZABETH II
ANDY WARHOL, 1985

Silkscreen print, 1000 x 800mm
NPG 5882(4)

This work was commissioned by *Reader's Digest* and presented to the National Portrait Gallery in celebration of the Queen's sixtieth birthday. Michael Leonard, a leading British photorealist painter, commented that his aim was 'a straightforward rather informal picture that would tend to play down the remoteness of Her Majesty's special position'. The corgi was 8-year-old Spark, whom the Queen herself chose to bring along to the sittings, 'possibly because of her obedience and good nature ... Spark was a great asset at the sittings. She did all that was asked of her and provided the occasion for Her Majesty to adopt a pose that was unforced and natural, lending the composition a degree of liveliness and movement.'

[53]
QUEEN ELIZABETH II
YELLOW DRAWING ROOM, BUCKINGHAM
PALACE, LONDON
MICHAEL LEONARD, 1985–6

Acrylic on canvas, 762 x 616mm
NPG 5861

Japanese artist Hiroshi Sugimoto's strangely
disconcerting portrait of the Queen actually
shows a wax mannequin. What appears to
be a photograph of a living human being is
revealed to be a photograph of a stiff and
artificial recreation, a wax figure whose
likeness was carefully modelled from other
photographic reproductions of the sitter:
a portrait three times removed from the
Queen herself. It forms part of a series
of photographs taken from wax effigies
and tableaux in public attractions such as
Madame Tussaud's, London.

[55]
QUEEN ELIZABETH II
HIROSHI SUGIMOTO, 1999

Gelatin silver print laid on aluminium,
1492 x 1194mm
NPG P1002

Commissioned by the National Portrait Gallery to celebrate the hundredth birthday of the Queen Mother, John Wonnacott's portrait of four generations of royals was suggested by the artist himself as a way of immortalising the royal family on the eve of a new millennium. The work shows, from left to right, Prince William; Queen Elizabeth II; Prince Philip, Duke of Edinburgh; Prince Harry; Prince Charles, Prince of Wales; and Queen Elizabeth, the Queen Mother, seated at the centre. The sitters are depicted in the White Drawing Room at Buckingham Palace, recalling Sir John Lavery's 1913 portrait of the family of George V, also in the Gallery's Collection (NPG 1745).

[57]
'THE ROYAL FAMILY: A CENTENARY PORTRAIT'
WHITE DRAWING ROOM, BUCKINGHAM PALACE, LONDON
JOHN WONNACOTT, 2000

Oil on canvas, 3663 x 2493mm
NPG 6479

The artist Lucian Freud was asked to paint the Queen wearing the Diamond Diadem Crown – the same one that she wore when photographed by Dorothy Wilding almost fifty years earlier (see p. 60). Sittings for the portrait took place at St James's Palace between May 2000 and September 2001, one of which is documented in this photograph by Freud's studio manager, David Dawson.

(see p. 60)

[58]
QUEEN ELIZABETH II
ST JAMES'S PALACE, LONDON
DAVID DAWSON, 2001

C-type colour print, 390 x 590mm
NPG x128570

[60]
QUEEN ELIZABETH II
BLUE DRAWING ROOM,
BUCKINGHAM PALACE, LONDON
JANE BOWN, 2006

Gelatin silver print, 318 x 480mm
NPG x133110

[61]
QUEEN ELIZABETH II
BUCKINGHAM PALACE, LONDON
ANNIE LEIBOVITZ, 2007

Chromogenic print, 864 x 1244mm
NPG P1315

Commissioned in 2004 by the island of Jersey, this portrait was made by Ontario-born artist Chris Levine with holographer Rob Munday to commemorate the island's 800-year allegiance to the Crown. Two sittings took place and over 10,000 images were made to create a three-dimensional portrait. *Equanimity* was the first holographic portrait of the Queen.

The National Portrait Gallery commissioned the German photographer Thomas Struth's portrait of Queen Elizabeth II and Prince Philip to mark the Queen's Diamond Jubilee in 2012. The couple are posed in the Green Drawing Room at Windsor Castle shortly before Prince Philip's ninetieth birthday, during what was the sixty-fourth year of their marriage. The portrait is a sensitive portrayal of the royal couple away from their official and ceremonial roles, but the splendid setting reminds the viewer of their status.

[63]
PRINCE PHILIP, DUKE OF EDINBURGH AND QUEEN ELIZABETH II
GREEN DRAWING ROOM, WINDSOR CASTLE, BERKSHIRE
THOMAS STRUTH, 7 APRIL 2011

Chromogenic print, 1633 x 2062mm
NPG P1665

TIMELINE

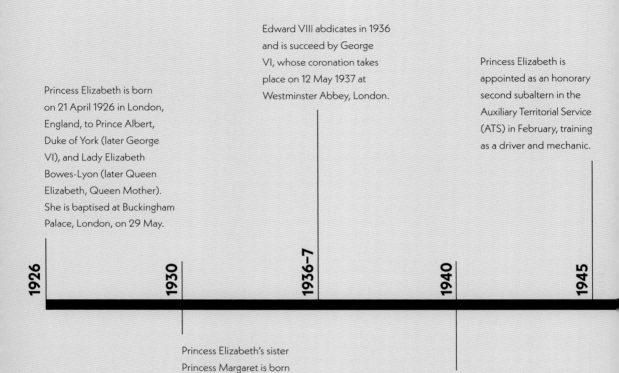

Princess Elizabeth is born on 21 April 1926 in London, England, to Prince Albert, Duke of York (later George VI), and Lady Elizabeth Bowes-Lyon (later Queen Elizabeth, Queen Mother). She is baptised at Buckingham Palace, London, on 29 May.

Edward VIII abdicates in 1936 and is succeed by George VI, whose coronation takes place on 12 May 1937 at Westminster Abbey, London.

Princess Elizabeth is appointed as an honorary second subaltern in the Auxiliary Territorial Service (ATS) in February, training as a driver and mechanic.

1926

1930

1936–7

1940

1945

Princess Elizabeth's sister Princess Margaret is born on 21 August.

On 13 October, Princess Elizabeth, joined by Princess Margaret, broadcasts a message on BBC's Children's Hour to the children of the Commonwealth evacuated from Britain during the Second World War.

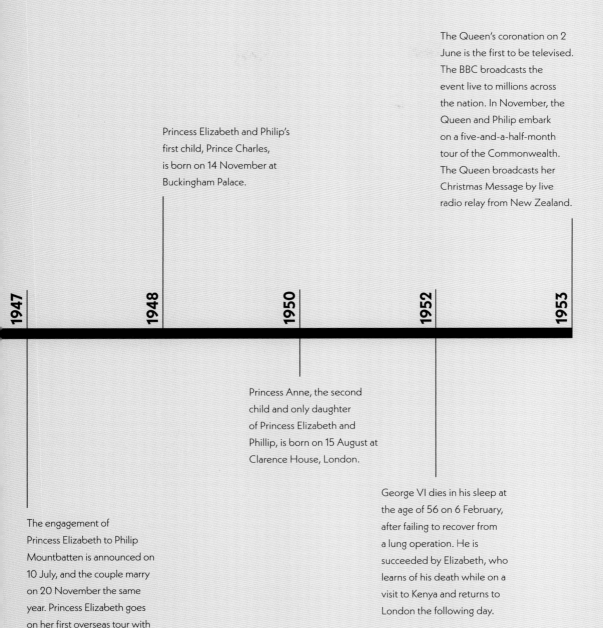

1947

1948

Princess Elizabeth and Philip's first child, Prince Charles, is born on 14 November at Buckingham Palace.

1950

1952

1953

The Queen's coronation on 2 June is the first to be televised. The BBC broadcasts the event live to millions across the nation. In November, the Queen and Philip embark on a five-and-a-half-month tour of the Commonwealth. The Queen broadcasts her Christmas Message by live radio relay from New Zealand.

Princess Anne, the second child and only daughter of Princess Elizabeth and Phillip, is born on 15 August at Clarence House, London.

George VI dies in his sleep at the age of 56 on 6 February, after failing to recover from a lung operation. He is succeeded by Elizabeth, who learns of his death while on a visit to Kenya and returns to London the following day.

The engagement of Princess Elizabeth to Philip Mountbatten is announced on 10 July, and the couple marry on 20 November the same year. Princess Elizabeth goes on her first overseas tour with her family, visiting South Africa.

The Queen and Philip return to London in May, having travelled over 40,000 miles during their tour of the Commonwealth.

The Queen announces that Prince Charles will be created Prince of Wales. She hosts the last presentation of debutantes at Buckingham Palace.

On 19 February Prince Andrew, the Queen and Prince Philip's third child, is born at Buckingham Palace.

1954

1957

1958

1959

1960

On 22 February, the Queen agrees that her husband's official title should include the title of a Prince, making him Prince Philip, Duke of Edinburgh. In October, the royal couple begin a state visit to the USA. At Christmas the Queen makes the first televised address to the nation.

In June and July the Queen and Prince Philip undertake a six-week tour of Canada.

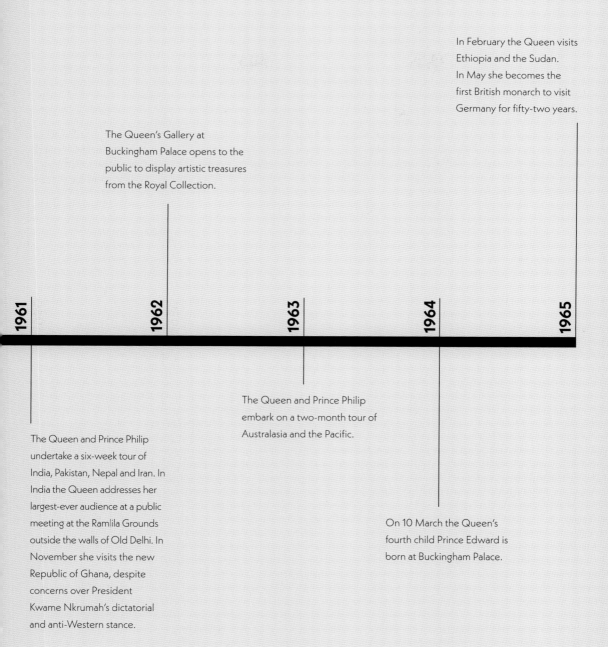

In February the Queen visits Ethiopia and the Sudan. In May she becomes the first British monarch to visit Germany for fifty-two years.

The Queen's Gallery at Buckingham Palace opens to the public to display artistic treasures from the Royal Collection.

1961

1962

1963

1964

1965

The Queen and Prince Philip embark on a two-month tour of Australasia and the Pacific.

The Queen and Prince Philip undertake a six-week tour of India, Pakistan, Nepal and Iran. In India the Queen addresses her largest-ever audience at a public meeting at the Ramlila Grounds outside the walls of Old Delhi. In November she visits the new Republic of Ghana, despite concerns over President Kwame Nkrumah's dictatorial and anti-Western stance.

On 10 March the Queen's fourth child Prince Edward is born at Buckingham Palace.

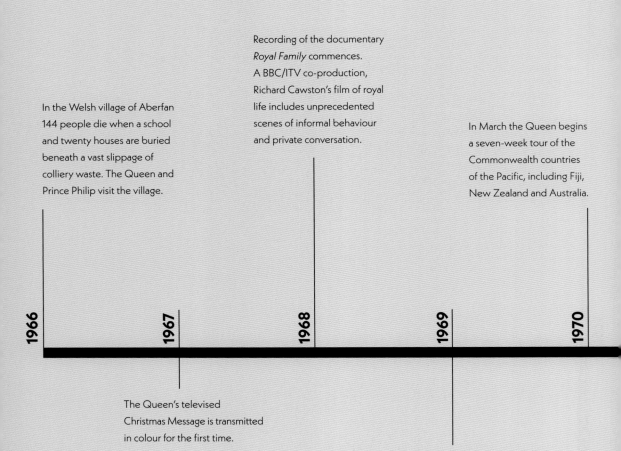

In the Welsh village of Aberfan 144 people die when a school and twenty houses are buried beneath a vast slippage of colliery waste. The Queen and Prince Philip visit the village.

Recording of the documentary *Royal Family* commences. A BBC/ITV co-production, Richard Cawston's film of royal life includes unprecedented scenes of informal behaviour and private conversation.

In March the Queen begins a seven-week tour of the Commonwealth countries of the Pacific, including Fiji, New Zealand and Australia.

1966

1967

1968

1969

1970

The Queen's televised Christmas Message is transmitted in colour for the first time.

Royal Family is transmitted for the first time in June. It is repeated over the next eighteen months and shown around the world. In the United Kingdom it attracts more than thirty million viewers.

The Queen tours southwest Asia. In May she visits her uncle, the Duke of Windsor (formerly King Edward VIII), who is terminally ill and dies on 28 May. The Queen's Silver Wedding anniversary is celebrated.

The Queen's Silver Jubilee is celebrated throughout the Commonwealth. She embarks on a tour of the United Kingdom, including Northern Ireland, despite the IRA threat. She visits thirty-six counties in three months. On 15 November she becomes a grandmother when Princess Anne gives birth to a son, Peter.

1971

1972

1973

1975

1977

Princess Anne marries Captain Mark Phillips. Britain becomes a member of the European Common Market, a development that carries implications for the Queen as Head of the Commonwealth.

A House of Commons select committee defines the Queen's official duties.

Ties with the Commonwealth are emphasised as the Queen institutes the Order of Australia and the Queen's Service Order, New Zealand.

The Canadian Prime Minister
Pierre Trudeau proposes
the transfer of the Queen's
functions to the Governor
General of Canada, while
retaining the title Queen of
Canada. This would lead to the
Canada Act, proclaimed by the
Queen in Canada in 1982.

On 24 February Buckingham
Palace announces the
engagement of Prince Charles
and Diana Spencer. Princess Anne
gives birth to her second child,
Zara, on 15 May. In June a 17-year-
old boy fires blanks at the Queen
while she is riding on horseback
during Trooping the Colour. On
29 July an international audience
of three-quarters of a billion
watches the royal wedding of
Prince Charles and Diana.

On 15 September Diana,
Princess of Wales, gives birth
to a second son, Prince Harry.

1978   **1979**   **1981**   **1982**   **1984**

The Queen visits Kuwait, Bahrain,
Saudi Arabia, Qatar, the United
Arab Emirates and Oman.

On 21 June Diana, Princess
of Wales, gives birth to a son,
Prince William. In July an
intruder breaks into the Queen's
bedroom at Buckingham Palace.

The press publish reports that
the Prince and Princess of Wales
are leading independent lives.
In June Prince Edward, the
Duke and Duchess of York, and
Princess Anne appear in *It's a
Royal Knockout*, a television
game show. Replacing decorum
with knockabout humour, the
programme is a watershed in the
public's perception of royalty.

In May the Queen becomes
the first British head of state to
address a joint meeting of the
US Congress in Washington.

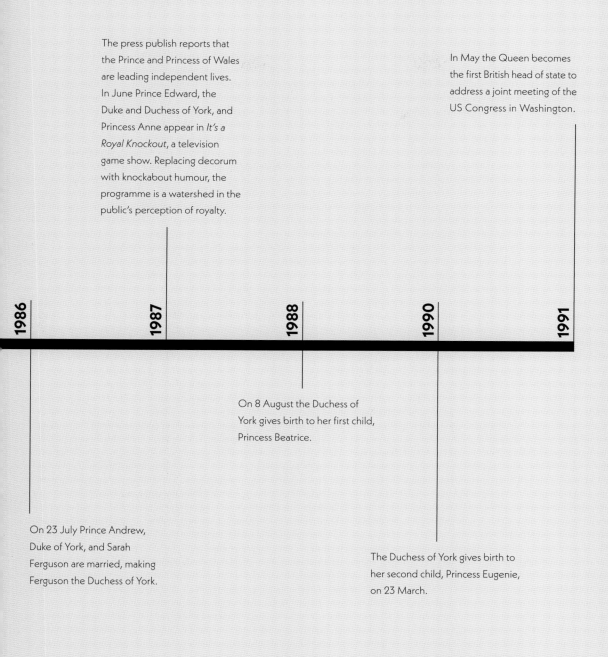

1986

1987

1988

1990

1991

On 8 August the Duchess of
York gives birth to her first child,
Princess Beatrice.

On 23 July Prince Andrew,
Duke of York, and Sarah
Ferguson are married, making
Ferguson the Duchess of York.

The Duchess of York gives birth to
her second child, Princess Eugenie,
on 23 March.

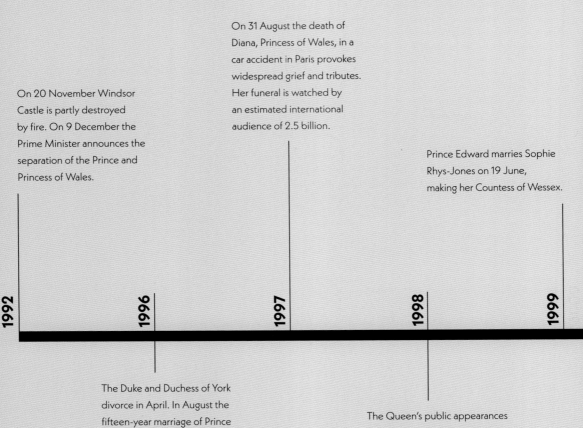

On 31 August the death of
Diana, Princess of Wales, in a
car accident in Paris provokes
widespread grief and tributes.
Her funeral is watched by
an estimated international
audience of 2.5 billion.

On 20 November Windsor
Castle is partly destroyed
by fire. On 9 December the
Prime Minister announces the
separation of the Prince and
Princess of Wales.

Prince Edward marries Sophie
Rhys-Jones on 19 June,
making her Countess of Wessex.

1992

1996

1997

1998

1999

The Duke and Duchess of York
divorce in April. In August the
fifteen-year marriage of Prince
Charles and Diana, Princess of
Wales, also ends in divorce.

The Queen's public appearances
demonstrate a move to greater
informality. During a state visit
to Brunei, her speeches refer
repeatedly to 'modernisation'.

The Queen attends official celebrations to mark the new millennium, including the opening of the Millennium Dome at Greenwich and religious services at Southwark and St Paul's cathedrals.

The Queen celebrates her eightieth birthday with a walkabout in Windsor town centre. She hosts a lunch for people also celebrating their eightieth birthday, a party for two thousand children at Buckingham Palace and a family dinner at Kew Palace.

Prince Edward's first child, Louise, is born on 8 November.

2000

2002

2003

2005

2006

The Queen celebrates her Golden Jubilee, marking fifty years since her accession. On 9 February Princess Margaret dies at the age of 71, following a stroke. On 30 March the Queen Mother dies aged 101.

On 8 April Prince Charles and Camilla Parker Bowles are married at Windsor Guildhall.

On 20 November the Queen and the Duke of Edinburgh celebrate their Diamond Wedding anniversary. Prince Edward's second child, James, is born on 17 December.

The Duke and Duchess of Cambridge's first child Prince George is born on 22 July. The Succession to the Crown Act ends the system of male primogeniture, under which a younger son can displace an elder daughter in the line of succession.

The Queen unveils a memorial statue in honour of the late Queen Mother on The Mall, London. She re-launches the British Monarchy website at Buckingham Palace.

2007

2009

2011

2013

2015

On 29 April Prince William and Catherine Middleton marry at Westminster Abbey, London, receiving the titles of Duke and Duchess of Cambridge. In June the Duke of Edinburgh celebrates his ninetieth birthday.

The Queen becomes the longest-reigning British monarch in history. In March the changes from the Succession to the Crown Act (2013) come into force. On 2 May, the Duke and Duchess of Cambridge's second child Princess Charlotte is born.

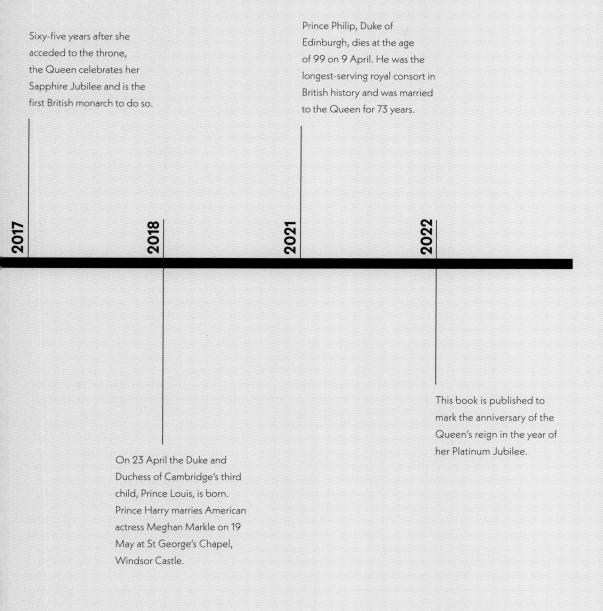

Sixy-five years after she acceded to the throne, the Queen celebrates her Sapphire Jubilee and is the first British monarch to do so.

Prince Philip, Duke of Edinburgh, dies at the age of 99 on 9 April. He was the longest-serving royal consort in British history and was married to the Queen for 73 years.

2017

2018

2021

2022

On 23 April the Duke and Duchess of Cambridge's third child, Prince Louis, is born. Prince Harry marries American actress Meghan Markle on 19 May at St George's Chapel, Windsor Castle.

This book is published to mark the anniversary of the Queen's reign in the year of her Platinum Jubilee.

SELECT BIBLIOGRAPHY

The captions accompanying the images draw on material from a range of National Portrait Gallery publications and online resources, with contributions made by curators Rosie Broadley, Sabina Jaskot-Gill and Clare Freestone. These sources are listed below with the page numbers of the relevant captions.

100 Photographs (2018): 114, 130

National Portrait Gallery: A Portrait of Britain (2014): 128

Cannadine, Sir David, *Tudors to Windsors: British Royal Portraits* (2018): 48, 60, 85, 119, 130

Gibson, Robin, *Pets in Portraits* (2015): 110

Howgate, Sarah; Auping, Michael (appreciation); Richardson, John (appreciation), *Lucian Freud: Portraits* (2012): 121

Moorhouse, Paul, *The Queen: Art and Image* (2011): 58, 60, 64, 78, 83, 91, 106, 114

Ribeiro, Aileen; Blackman, Cally, *A Portrait of Fashion: Six Centuries of Dress at the National Portrait Gallery* (2015): 48

Williamson, David, *Kings and Queens* (2010): 110

npg.org.uk: 28, 48, 60, 68, 106, 110, 114, 119, 128

PICTURE CREDITS

Front cover, p.52 Purchased, 1991.
Back cover, p.129 Portrait by Chris Levine (Artist) Rob Munday (Holographer). Commissioned by The Jersey Heritage Trust to commemorate the Island of Jersey's 800 years of allegiance to the English crown. 2004. Given by The People of Jersey, 2012.
p.2 (detail) Purchased, 1991.
p.6 Given by Public appeal, 1973.
p.8 © Photo by Lisa Sheridan/Studio Lisa/Getty Images.
p.9 Photograph © David Montgomery. Given by Peter Fetterman Gallery, 2019.
p.10, p.87 Given by Sir Hugh Leggatt, 1970.
p.11 Given by Terence Pepper, 2014.
p.12 © William Hustler and Georgina Hustler/National Portrait Gallery, London. Given by the photographer's sister, Susan Morton, 1976.
p.13 Lichfield/Lichfield Collection/Getty Images. Purchased, 1986.
p.14 (detail) © estate of Marcus Adams/Camera Press. Purchased, 1980.
p.19 Given by Fraser Robinson on behalf of Ian Lucas (from the collection of Ethel Keide).
p.21 Given by Terence Pepper, 2014.
p.23 © estate of Marcus Adams/Camera Press. Purchased, 1980.
p.25, p.26 Given by Terence Pepper, 2014.
p.27 © William Hustler and Georgina Hustler/National Portrait Gallery, London. Given by the photographer's sister, Susan Morton, 1976.
p.29 © estate of Marcus Adams/Camera Press. Purchased, 1980.
p.31 © Photo by Lisa Sheridan/Studio Lisa/Getty Images.
p.33 © Cecil Beaton/Victoria and Albert Museum, London. Given by Cecil Beaton, 1977.
p.37 © Cecil Beaton/Victoria and Albert Museum, London. Purchased, 1981.
p.38 © William Hustler and Georgina Hustler/National Portrait Gallery, London. Given by the photographer's sister, Susan Morton, 1976.
p.39 © reserved; collection National Portrait Gallery, London.
p.41 © William Hustler and Georgina Hustler/National Portrait Gallery, London. Purchased, 1991.

p.43 © William Hustler and Georgina Hustler/National Portrait Gallery, London. Purchased, 1991.

p.44 © Cecil Beaton/Victoria and Albert Museum, London. Acquired from Eileen Hose, 1986.

p.45 © Baron/Camera Press.

p.47 © estate of Bertram Park/National Portrait Gallery, London. Transferred from Hulton Picture Library, 1986.

p.49 Commissioned, 1950.

p.50 © reserved; collection National Portrait Gallery, London. Purchased, 1990.

p.51 © Karsh/Camera Press. Given by the photographer, Yousuf Karsh, 1987.

p.57, p.59 Given by the photographer's sister, Susan Morton, 1976.

p.60 © William Hustler and Georgina Hustler/National Portrait Gallery, London. Given by the photographer's sister, Susan Morton, 1976.

p.61 © William Hustler and Georgina Hustler/National Portrait Gallery, London. Given by the photographer's sister, Susan Morton, 1976.

p.63 © Baron/Camera Press. Given by Mr Ford Hill and the American Friends of the National Portrait Gallery (London) Foundation, Inc., 2015.

p.65 © Cecil Beaton/Victoria and Albert Museum, London. Acquired from the estate of Cecil Beaton, 1986 in conjunction with the *Elizabeth II* exhibition.

p.67 Purchased, 1977.

p.69 Contributor: Trinity Mirror/Mirrorpix/Alamy Stock Photo. Given by Mirrorpix, 2012.

p.71 Photograph by Tony Armstrong Jones © Armstrong Jones with thanks to Camera Press. Given by Mr Ford Hill and the American Friends of the National Portrait Gallery (London) Foundation, Inc., 2015.

p.73 © Camera Press Ltd; On loan from American Friends of the National Portrait Gallery (London) Foundation, Inc.: Gift of Mr. Ford Hill. Given by Mr Ford Hill and the American Friends of the National Portrait Gallery (London) Foundation, Inc., 2015.

p.74 © Camera Press. Given by Mr Ford Hill and the American Friends of the National Portrait Gallery (London) Foundation, Inc., 2015.

p.75 © reserved; collection National Portrait Gallery, London. Given by John Plimmer, 1977.

p.76 © Karsh/Camera Press. Given by the photographer, Yousuf Karsh, 1987.

p.77 © Karsh/Camera Press; On loan from American Friends of the National Portrait Gallery (London) Foundation, Inc.: Gift of Mr. Ford Hill. Given by Mr Ford Hill and the American Friends of the National Portrait Gallery (London) Foundation, Inc., 2015.

p.79 Photograph © David Montgomery. Given by Peter Fetterman Gallery, 2019.

p.81 Lichfield/Lichfield Collection/Getty Images. Given by Thomas Patrick John Anson, 5th Earl of Lichfield, 2003 in conjunction with the exhibition *Lichfield: the Early Years 1962–1982*.

p.82 © Eve Arnold/Magnum Photos. Purchased, 1993.

pp.84–5 © Joan Williams. Given by Joan Williams, 2015.

p.89 Lichfield/Lichfield Collection/Getty Images. Purchased, 1986.

p.90 Lichfield/Lichfield Collection/Getty Images. Acquired from Thomas Patrick John Anson, 5th Earl of Lichfield, 1986.

p.93 Lichfield/Lichfield Collection/Getty Images; On loan from American Friends of the National Portrait Gallery (London) Foundation, Inc.: Gift of Mr. Ford Hill. Given by Mr Ford Hill and the American Friends of the National Portrait Gallery (London) Foundation, Inc., 2015.

p.94 © CAVOUK Portraits. Given by Mr Ford Hill and the American Friends of the National Portrait Gallery (London) Foundation, Inc., 2015.

p.97 © Andrew Davidson; Camera Press. Purchased, 1975.

p.99 © Camera Press Ltd; On loan from American Friends of the National Portrait Gallery (London) Foundation, Inc.: Gift of Mr. Ford Hill. Given by Mr Ford Hill and the American Friends of the National Portrait Gallery (London) Foundation, Inc., 2015.

p.101 BBC Photo Library. Given by Joan Williams, 2015.

p.102 © Chris Levine. Purchased, 2013.

pp.106–9 © 2021 The Andy Warhol Foundation for the Visual Arts, Inc./Licensed by DACS, London. Purchased, 1986.

p.111 Given by Reader's Digest Association, 1986.

p.113 © Karsh/Camera Press. Given by the photographer, Yousuf Karsh, 1993.

p.115 © Hiroshi Sugimoto. Purchased, 2003.

p.117 © David Secombe. Purchased, 2002.

p.118 © John Wonnacott/National Portrait Gallery, London. Commissioned, 2000.

p.121 © David Dawson. Given by John Morton Morris, 2006.

p.123 © Anthony Crickmay/Camera Press. Purchased, 2002.

pp.124–5 © The Jane Bown Literary Estate/National Portrait Gallery, London. Purchased, 2009.

pp.126–7 © Annie Leibovitz/Trunk Archive. Given by Annie Leibovitz, 2008.

pp.130–1 © Thomas Struth, 2011. Commissioned, 2011.

p.133 © Jason Bell. Purchased, 2014.

p.135 © David Bailey. Commissioned and given by the GREAT Britain Campaign, 2015.

Published in Great Britain by
National Portrait Gallery Publications
National Portrait Gallery
St Martin's Place
London WC2H 0HE

Every purchase supports the National
Portrait Gallery, London. For a complete
catalogue of current publications, please visit
our website at www.npg.org/publications

Text pp.7–13 by Alexandra Shulman, written
in July 2021.

Front cover: *Queen Elizabeth II* by Dorothy
Wilding, 26 February 1952

Back cover: *Equanimity* by Chris Levine
(Artist) Rob Munday (Holographer), 2012

ISBN 978-1-85514-743-0

A catalogue record for this book is available
from the British Library.

10 9 8 7 6 5 4

Director of Commercial: Anna Starling
Publishing Manager: Kara Green
Project Editor: Tijana Todorinovic
Picture Library Manager: Mark Lynch
Publishing Executive: Tom Love
Design: Daniela Rocha
Printed in Italy by Printer Trento
Origination by DL Imaging